Thank You to my family for encouraging and helping me along the way and to the friends and co-workers that shared their points of view.

To all my students and one in particular, who even has her own debut in this book. You know who you are, **Thank You!**

Thank you to the readers and to the Caterpillars who dared to become Butterflies!~

For orders or requests contact the publisher at helloreaders@thecolorofstories.com.
Cover and illustrations by Sequoia Bostick
Hardcover: 978-1-7355422-1-8
Paperback: 978-1-7355422-0-1
Ebook: 978-1-7355422-2-5

Library of Congress Number: 2020925290
Mims, Martinique

Through the Colors of a Butterfly

You are made in **Uniqueness** and in love.

Unique could not believe her family was going to move. "Momma, what about my friends? I love them so much; I don't want to leave!" said Unique.

"Honey, I understand, but you can still visit your friends. Plus, this is going to be a great adventure. Trust me, you'll see," said Momma.

On the way to her new home Unique could only think about all the things she would miss: being captain of the soccer team, winning school spirit week with her wacky tacky costumes, being a leader for class assignments, and most of all, her friends.

Mom and Star were laughing and talking in the car. But all the while, going to school the next day lurked in the back of Unique's mind. She was worried no one would like her or maybe she wouldn't like them.

After settling in their new home, the next morning, Momma cooked a special breakfast, but Unique wanted to hide and couldn't eat a single bite. Her stomach flipped and flopped. Meanwhile, Star scarfed down all of her waffles and Unique's waffles too! She was excited to go to a new school.

"It's going to be okay, Unique. Just be yourself. That's what I'm going to do," said Star. Unique rolled her eyes and said, "But what if they don't like me, because I'm different? Going to third grade in the middle of the year is no good."

When Unique arrived at her new school, her teacher, Ms. Mangu welcomed her. "Unique, we're so excited to have you! In my class, everyone shares their favorite color. What's yours?" she asked.

Math

Social Studies

Science

But Unique did not say a word, she just shuffled her feet. "That's okay," said the teacher, "You can share another time. You're welcome to have a seat at your new desk."

It had only been five minutes and already Unique felt she didn't belong. The other students raised their hands before she could and talked to one another so easily. "I don't know anything about this school and no one likes me," thought Unique.

At recess, Unique wanted to play soccer, but she was afraid her new classmates might not want her to play. She felt different and not so good. "I thought I was special, but I'm not unique. **Not. At. All.**"

After Recess, Ms. Mangu called on her. "Unique, what do you think about butterflies?" she asked. Unique was still afraid to speak. "I don't think she knows how to talk, Ms. Mangu," said one student. Unique sank lower in her seat.

"That's okay, maybe you're not quite ready to share your thoughts," said Ms. Mangu.

"But you came to our class on an exciting day, we are selecting a very lucky student to take our special classroom pet home for two weeks!"

"And because I love new beginnings, that lucky student will be...

UNIQUE!

Unique shook her head NO. Everyone looked at her.
She didn't feel lucky at all.

"Wonderful. Unique, you get to take home our pet friend, Pillar, the caterpillar. Then, in two weeks, you will share your observations with the entire class," Ms. Mangu said enthusiastically.

Unique, trying hard not to trip, walked to the front of the class and silently took the jar. She couldn't believe she had to take care of a worm for two whole weeks, and, even worse, talk about it in front of the whole class!

"What am I supposed to do with a worm?"
Unique asked Star when she got home.

"That's not a worm, it's a caterpillar. This is going to be magical,
Unique. You just wait and see," said Star.

Unique sat and stared at the worm. "I don't see what's so special about you," she whispered. Still, every day she gave it a big juicy leaf and water...

and kept it warm by the window.

Until one day, something happened. Pillar had wrapped himself up tight. The caterpillar had turned into a cocoon! "Why is he hiding?" she asked aloud.

Then days passed and nothing interesting happened. Until one day, Unique saw the cocoon had been broken open, and nothing was inside.

Unique opened the lid to the jar and out flew a beautiful butterfly!

All through the night...

Pillar's wings fluttered, creating a big color cloud in the room.

Then in a haze Unique found herself standing on a tree branch. She couldn't believe her eyes — **she was in a forest and was as small as a pen top!**

All of a sudden, she felt a gust of wind as a ginormous butterfly flew towards her. It was Pillar!

He motioned for her to hop on for a ride. Suddenly, Pillar's colors began to change and so did the world around them.

Blue water and skies reflect how helpful, thoughtful and caring Unique is to her friends and family.

Purple for power and creativity; Unique has power within herself.

Unique's whole world turns the color of the butterfly's wings.

Yellow for how happy and silly she can be, bringing joy to those around her.

And pink for the kindness and compassion she gives others.

Pillar returned Unique back to the large oak. THEN...Pillar spoke!

"Unique, you have many gifts. Don't hide in a cocoon. Let everyone see who you really are. Shine, shine, shine!"

"But what if they don't like me because i'm different." Unique asked.

"Don't hold back just because you may be different. Those colors represent each part of you and just know you too can be a butterfly!" said Pillar. Then just like that, he flew away.

Unique woke up filled with joy and couldn't wait to get to school!

She walked into third grade with a beaming smile.

The students looked at Unique differently because she had on more than just a beautiful outfit, she had on **confidence!**

OBJECTIVES

Reading
Writing
Math
Social Studies
Science

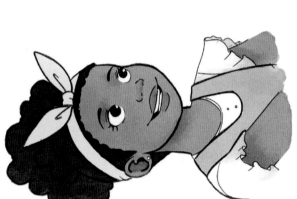

She's not afraid to show off her soccer skills at recess!

and she talks to students she never spoke to before.

Ms. Mangu asked Unique to share what she learned about their friend, Pillar. Unique takes a breath and walks to the front of the room and said...

"Through the colors of a butterfly, I fell into a dream.
I heard the flutter of wings, breathed the air and flowers around me.

I discovered the gifts and amazing things I bring.
I admire you but will never forget what I can do too.

Through the colors of a butterfly, I am **Unique**.

I don't have to hide or choose not to speak.
That's no good for you or me.

I am **beautiful** and different and that's okay.
No one is just alike, we all have beauty we can bring.

Through the colors of a butterfly, I **believe** in me."

When she finished, the class cheered and the teacher beamed. "Thank you so much, Unique. It's great to hear your voice in our class.

Now it's time for us to let
our friend, Pillar, fly free.

"Good-bye Pillar. Thank you," whispered Unique as she opened the lid and let Pillar fly off. The students cheered. Unique now realized that her school was not so bad, and through her own colors she has something unique to bring.

THE END

Each and every one of us is uniquely beautiful and has a gift that can be shared with the world!

God made you **Unique**. I praise you because I am fearfully and wonderfully made; your works are wonderful, I know that full well.

Psalm 139:14

Author
Note from the Author

We are for ever-growing, learning, and changing. We can always learn something new about ourselves and those around us. Continue to plant seeds of love, generosity, and kindness in fertile soil. Always remember YOU are Uniquely, Wonderfully, and Beautifully made. I hope you enjoyed this story!
~Keep reading!

Monarch Butterflies

We must care for our friends in nature.

Did you know:
In 2020 Monarch Butterflies were listed on the endangered species list!

Nectar and water are tasted by the sensory hairs on a butterfly's legs and feet.

Monarch butterflies are known to travel 3,000 miles each year to reach their winter home!

Growing native plant gardens at home is one way to help support the population of the monarch butterfly.

In the fall of 2019, Martinique saw 2 to 3 butterflies every day which inspired the idea for this story!

Visit National Geographic for more facts on this species!

Learning about Differences

"Talking to children about disabilities can help them better understand themselves and their peers."

Everyone has differences, take time to discuss what qualities make you Unique!

"Everyone is different—some people have glasses, some have freckles or curly hair. Even if a child performs daily tasks differently, make sure children understand that this does not make them less valuable."

Our character, Unique was born without her left leg and wears what is called a prosthetic-this is designed to help someone get around more easily.

Visit BioAdvance Prosthetic Solutions and Enabling Devices.com for more info on this topic

THE AUTHOR

Martinique Mims is a slam poet and children's book author who writes while looking through the lens of history & the triumphs & challenges people face, especially communities of color. Her goal is t uplift children through her stories & encourage them to be who they are & to realize they can & should share the gifts God gave them.

Her stories have a purpose: to help young people build up self-esteem, to encourage them to believe in themselves even if they may feel different, & to find joy within themselves. She wants her books be a great escape, a place for children to imagine and believe anything is possible.

When she is not busy writing, Martinique likes to go to local ice cream shops or smoothie cafe's & try all kinds of flavors. She enjoy: dancing, singing, & finding new styles for her natural hair (which she loves). This is her debut children's book.

🌐 thecolorofstories.com

📷 @thecolorofstories10

f thecolorofstories10

THE ARTIST

Sequoia Bostick is an Illustrator, maker, & designer living in Cleveland, Ohio. After earning her BFA in Illustration from the Cleveland Institute of Art in 2014, she pursued a career as a resider teaching artist where she works with local youth to grow their visual art skills all while growing her own artistic practice as a multi-disciplinary freelancer. She is a project oriented artist & loves worki with others on large assignments.

Sequoia's work has been featured in Cleveland Scene Magazine, Vagabond Comics, Ideastream, The CAN Journal, & The Plain Dealer. You can also find her work in Cleveland Botanical Gardens, The Cleveland Museum of Art, & Maelstrom Collaborative Arts.

When she's not making art, She loves taking care of plants, going on long hikes, biking, and playing video games.

🌐 sequoiabostickart.com

📷 @sequoiabostickillustration

✉ sequoiabostick@gmail.com

Made in the USA
Monee, IL
03 March 2021